Columbia University

Contributions to Education

Teachers College Series

No. 152

AMS PRESS
NEW YORK

A STUDY OF INTELLIGENCE TEST ELEMENTS

BY

LEONA VINCENT, Ph.D.

Teachers College, Columbia University
Contributions Education, No. 152

Published by
Teachers College, Columbia University
New York City
1924

Library of Congress Cataloging in Publication Data

Vincent, Elizabeth Lee, 1897-
   A study of intelligence test elements.

   Reprint of the 1924 ed., issued in series: Teachers
College, Columbia University. Contributions to edu-
cation, no. 152.
   Originally presented as the author's thesis, Columbia.

   Bibliography: p.
   1. Mental tests. I. Title. II. Series: Columbia
University. Teachers College. Contributions to
education, no. 152.
LB1131.V5 1972   153.9'3   70-177675
ISBN 0-404-55152-1

Reprinted by Special Arrangement with Teachers
College Press, New York, New York

From the edition of 1924, New York
First AMS edition published in 1972
Manufactured in the United States

AMS PRESS, INC.
NEW YORK, N. Y.   10003

ACKNOWLEDGMENTS

The writer is indebted to the Institute of Educational Research of Teachers College for the original test records and scores used in this investigation. The collection of these records and scores was made possible by a grant to the Institute from the Carnegie Corporation.

The writer is very grateful to Professor A. I. Gates and to Professor William Bagley for guidance and inspiration, and deeply indebted to Professor E. L. Thorndike, to Professor Godfrey Thomson and to Professor William McCall, for the many hours of conference without which this work could not have been done.

This occasion is taken to express sincere appreciation to the members of the Institute of Educational Research, and especially to Miss Ella Woodyard, for the friendly coöperation which has made work in the Institute a pleasure.

E. L. V.

CONTENTS

INDEX TO TABLES

A STUDY OF INTELLIGENCE TEST ELEMENTS

CHAPTER I

INTRODUCTION

The history of mental tests is a long one. Plato (translated by Jowett, '88) suggested that youths should be selected according to their abilities, stated the qualifications which he considered necessary for each position to be filled, and definitely mentioned (p. 203) that "the aspirant must . . . be tested." He offered, however, no specific test suggestions.

It was not until the nineteenth century that experimental psychology and the study of mental processes came into general prominence. In the first stages of this scientific development, there existed an "erroneous presupposition that any psychological method of experimentation would be really usable as a test." (Stern, '12, p. 14.) As a result there was considerable misuse of experimental methods. From this condition it was revived by Binet, and a significant advance was made when "it was finally recognized that (this) blind probing about could not lead us farther," and, "that on the contrary, tests of intelligence must be definitely selected." (Stern, '12, p. 15.)

The newer movement then sought for exact methods of experimentation which would "bring intelligence into direct and manifest operation." (Stern, '12, p. 15.) It is the spirit of this "directness" which is guiding the more recent work in intelligence measurement, and, following the development of usable tests, the general direction has been toward their perfection. Such attempts as those of Spearman and Burt, to analyze the *thing measured,* have given way to more practical efforts to perfect the *methods of measurement.* Such efforts are represented by the studies of Wyatt, Kelley, McCall, Gates, and Herring, all of which have contributed to the knowledge of "what is the more intelligent

1

process?" and, "of what practical use is measurement?" In line with these are the work of Ebbinghaus and that of Trabue, which carry still further the analysis of special mental processes.

It seems from the general trend of these studies that the next step in the improvement of tests of intelligence should consist of an analysis of test elements, the smaller unit reactions which go to make up the various test reactions. As yet no method has been developed for facilitating such an analysis. The object of this investigation is, in part, a study of method and, in part, an analysis of elements.

CHAPTER II

THE DATA

DEFINITION OF TERMS

A *test element* is used here to mean a sentence of a completion test, a problem in arithmetic, a question to be answered in reading. It cannot mean the elemental stimulus-response bonds which go to make up a unit reaction, but must, since an analysis of reactions into bonds is not as yet feasible, mean the unit reactions themselves.

The word *test* is used to mean a collection of elements of the same general content; for example, the arithmetic test is a group of arithmetic problems, the completion test is a group of sentences to be completed, and so on.

The *criterion* in the primary study is the total score on the Thorndike Intelligence Examination for High School Graduates, and, in the supplementary study with sixth grade children, it is the total score on a combination of tests which was found by the Institute of Educational Research of Teachers College to correlate highly with other measures of intelligence.[1]

The term *intelligence* is used without regard to the philosophical and psychological disputes which are at present current. It is used simply as a convenient term to cover that ability which is measured by the two tests, the total scores of which are used as the criteria. In the primary investigation the study is limited to such ability as presents itself for college entrance examination; in the supplementary investigation, to such ability as was found in the several sixth grades in New York public schools in December, 1923.

---

[1] The reliability of the Thorndike test is .85 (see Wood '23). The validity as measured against academic success in Columbia College (the unit was average grade multiplied by the number of points carried) is .59. Academic failures in the first semester had an average Thorndike score of 69; men who survived the first semester had an average score of 86. The Thorndike test in its 1922 form has 439 elements, and uses a total working time of 160 minutes. It includes language ability tests, mathematics, information, reading, trade tests, completion, and logic.

The test used for the sixth grade group was a combination of completion tests, arithmetic problems, word knowledge, speed of reading, and an I.E.R. intelligence test.

The *CBL group* is the Columbia-Barnard-Law group and is composed of examinations given to applicants for entrance into Columbia College and Barnard College of Columbia University in January, June, and September of each year from September, 1919, through January, 1924, and the applicants for entrance to the Law School of Columbia University in April and November of 1922 and December of 1923. The group includes the examinations of candidates who were rejected as well as of those who were accepted for entrance to the university.

The *S group* is made up of examinations given by the Institute of Educational Research in December, 1923, to a number of sixth grade children in the public schools of New York. Cases of specific English disability were excluded from the group with which this investigation concerns itself.

THE MATERIAL USED

The material used in this investigation consisted of elements in completion, arithmetic, and reading. It was made available through the Institute of Educational Research, by the kindness of Professor Thorndike. The intelligence examinations had been given, the blanks scored, and in many cases the scores of the elements tabulated before this particular study began. The elements had also been ranked for difficulty on the basis of per cents of passes for each element; for example, if the element was passed by 15 per cent of the people who took it, the ranking was G; if passed by 85 per cent, C, and so on. These letters represent degrees of difficulty, assuming the form of distribution of candidates for admission to Columbia University is approximately that of the normal probability curve. They were so chosen that an "E" or an "F" element in arithmetic is passed by the same percentage of people of a definite level of intelligence, as is an "E" or an "F" element in reading or completion. Table I shows more clearly the meaning of the key letters.

The percentages of passes for the elements studied in this investigation were based upon the same cases (the CBL group) as were used in this study. The frequencies of these cases are shown in Table III. The difficulty rankings are necessarily tentative and subject to improvement as the material available is increased. The samplings were for the most part large, however, and it seems quite probable that in the final classification few

TABLE I

MEANING OF LETTER RANKINGS

Letter Ranking of the Element	Percentage of Passes Among Those Who Took the Element as Part of a Test
H	5.5– 8.0
G	13.5–18.5
F	27.5–34.5
E	46.0–54.0
D	65.0–72.5
C	81.5–86.5
B	92.0–94.5
A	97.5–98.2

elements will be shifted from their present classification by more than one step in either direction, and quite improbable that any element now accounted very easy will later be shown to be very hard or vice versa.

The elements for the CBL group were distributed according to difficulty[2] and content, as shown in Table IIa. The S group were distributed as shown in Table IIb.

The material in the Institute of Educational Research available for the study of these particular elements was as nearly as possible exhausted. Since each of the examinations given to the CBL group was made up of different forms of the tests, it was neces-

TABLE IIA

DISTRIBUTION OF CBL ELEMENTS ACCORDING TO DIFFICULTY

Difficulty	Number of Elements in		
	Completion	Arithmetic	Reading
H	17	2	4
G	30	20	11
F	30	29	24
E	27	25	33
D	9	25	30
C	9	16	14
B	...	9	3
A	...	5	2
Totals	122	131	121

[2] These difficulty rankings do not hold for any other than a college entrance group.

TABLE IIв

DISTRIBUTION OF S ELEMENTS ACCORDING TO DIFFICULTY

Difficulty	Number of Elements in	
	Completion	Arithmetic
D	..	6
C	9	17
B	10	..
A	8	..
AA*............	..	10
AAA*............	..	10
Totals	27	43

* Easier editions than the Columbia A.

sary to trace the material for each element through its somewhat complicated appearances and reappearances. This meant that the number of cases for each element varied. Table III shows how the number of elements for each content was distributed according to the number of cases studied.

TABLE III

DISTRIBUTION OF ELEMENTS ACCORDING TO
NUMBER OF CASES STUDIED

Number of Cases	Number of Elements in Completion		Number of Elements in Arithmetic		Number of Elements in Reading
	CBL	S	CBL	S	CBL
50– 69	3	..	14	..	24
70– 89	6	..	28	..	35
90–109	5	..	23	..	11
110–129	8	..	6	..	2
130–149	15	..	...	10	43
150–174	11	9	9	23	6
175–199	5	9	5	..	...
200–224	26	..	4	..	...
225–249	12	..	1	10	...
250–274	4	..	13	..	...
275–299	7	..	5	..	...
300–349	13	..	14	..	...
350–399	4	9	7	..	...
400–449	1	..	1	..	...
450–499	2	..	1	..	...
Totals	122	27	131	43	121

CHAPTER III

THE METHOD

The initial tryout of methods used for the most part as its material the 122 elements in the completion tests. In a study of test elements, a criterion against which to measure the goodness of the element must be chosen. That criterion may be the total score on the test which includes the element as a part; it may be a subjective ranking of the intelligence of the individual to whom the test element is given; it may be the score on some combination of tests; or it may be any one of a number of possibilities. The general tendency in choosing criteria seems to be to favor the more objective. In this study the criterion chosen was the total score on the test which included in each case the element under consideration. This meant that the criterion in the CBL group was the total score on the Thorndike Intelligence Test for High School Graduates, a test which was made up of a combination of 439 elements.

In no case did the score on the element have more than six possibilities. On the completion and reading elements, the scores might have been $+3$, $+2$, $+1$, 0, -1, or -2; on arithmetic, $+4$, $+3$, $+2$, $+1$, or 0. On the other hand, the criterion against which the element scores were correlated[1] varied over a range of scores from 20 to 120. It is in studying the relation of a variable of so few categories with one of so many that the chief problem of method arises.

The first idea that occurs to one in thinking of relationship is the Pearson product-moment coefficient of correlation.[2]

Such coefficients were computed for 56 elements in completion, with frequencies ranging from 100 to 320. A critical survey of

---

[1] Correlated is here used as having any relation whatever.

[2] $r = \dfrac{\Sigma xy}{N\sigma x\sigma y}$ where X represents scores on the element, and Y scores on the total test, x being the deviation of the X's from the average X, and y the deviation of the Y's from the average Y. See Rugg, '17, p. 265; Kelley, '23, p. 171; Yule, '22, p. 202; Brown and Thomson, '23, p. 109; Thorndike, '04, p. 173.

the resulting r's showed that the probable errors were very large, and the correlations limited in range. It was apparent that the categories were too broad in the case of the element scores to make this method of studying the data a usable one.

The correction for broad categories was tried. The procedure[3] is not a simple one, and when applied changed the r by a small figure in the second decimal place only. It proved to be a cumbersome correction for an ill-fitting method.

Pearson's mean square contingency coefficient (Yule, '22, pp. 63-65) was considered, but in order to make its use practicable, the criterion scores would have to be condensed into a few groups. To do this would be to lose much of the discriminating power of the criterion.

A study of the keys by which the elements were scored showed that there was very little difference between the $+3$ and the $+2$ answers, and between the $+1$, the 0, the -1, and the -2 answers; but a considerable difference between the $+3$ and $+2$ and the $+1$, 0, -1, and -2 answers. In the weighting for difficulty mentioned above (p. 4) the Institute of Educational Research had considered the $+3$ and $+2$ scores as passed, and the $+1$, 0, -1, and -2 as failed. It seemed advisable, then, to consider the element scores as a dichotomous variable, with only the two possible scores, (1) pass and (2) failure.

This opened the way to new methods. Yule's coefficient of association (Yule, '22, p. 38) was cast aside because it implies dichotomy in both variables, and, as before, it did not seem wise to lose the discriminating power that the long variation in criterion scores would give. For the same reason the tetrachoric r (Kelley, '23, pp. 253-258) was rejected.

The obvious method to use in the case of correlation of a dichotomous variable with a many-categoried variable, is the method of bi-serial correlation. Thirty-five of these correlations with the P.E.'s were computed. (See Table IV.)[4]

---

[3] For the explanation of the method, the writer is indebted to Professor Thomson.

[4] (Kelley, '23, pp. 245-249.) $r = \dfrac{M_2 - M_1}{\sigma} \times \dfrac{pq}{z}$ where M_2 is the mean total score of the passes, M_1 of the failures; σ is the root mean square deviation of all the total scores for the elements (both passes and failures); p is the per cent of passes; q is the per cent of failures; z is the ordinate of the

In the meantime, the method of overlapping (Thorndike, '04, pp. 128-132) suggested itself. This is a method of comparing two groups which have a range of comparable scores, by finding the median of one group and computing the percentage of the second group which reaches or exceeds that median. Such a measure has probably not heretofore been used as a correlation method in the sense in which it is used in this study, but it seemed not unwise to try it. In this case, the two groups of scores under consideration were (1) the total test scores of those who passed an element, and (2) the total test scores of those who failed it. The application of the method is simple enough: Find the median total test score of the people who passed the element; find how many of the people who failed the element have total test scores which reach or exceed that median; find what per cent that number is of the total number of people who failed the element. Although it takes no small amount of time to do this, the time expended is rather less than that needed for computation of the bi-serial r, and if it could be proved that the method of overlapping picks out poor and good elements as well as does the bi-serial method, the study of many more elements would be made possible. With a comparison of the two methods in view, the overlapping percentages (referred to throughout this study as "overlappings" or "Omds")[5] were computed for the thirty-five completion elements for which the bi-serial r had previously been found. The two measures were tabulated in pairs and are shown in Table IV.

---

normal probability curve at the point where p per cent of the curve lies above and q per cent below (found from the table in Appendix C of Kelley's book). For example:

If $M_2 = 85$; $M_1 = 70$; $p = 25\%$; $q = 75\%$.

σ (of the total distribution of total scores) $= 13$.

z (from the table) $= .31777$

pq (also from the table) $= .187500$

$$\frac{M_2 - M_1}{\sigma} \times \frac{pq}{z} = \frac{85 - 70}{13} \times \frac{.1875}{.31777} = \frac{15}{13} \times .59005 = + .68092$$

$$r = + .681$$

$$\text{P.E. bi-serial} = \frac{.67449}{\sqrt{N}} \left(\frac{\sqrt{pq}}{z} - r^2 \right)$$

[5] There is no conventional justification for the adoption of this symbol.

TABLE IV

Overlappings and Bi-serial r's
for 35 Elements

Overlappings	Bi-serial r's with P.E.'s
0.0	.826 ± .046
5.2	.752 ± .049
6.4	.726 ± .046
8.9	.588 ± .057
9.1	.639 ± .054
10.0	.406 ± .082
11.7	.431 ± .083
12.3	.558 ± .061
12.4	.559 ± .068
12.5	.463 ± .068
12.6	.559 ± .060
15.2	.551 ± .048
15.8	.597 ± .061
16.5	.542 ± .041
18.7	.665 ± .031
20.7	.520 ± .037
21.2	.475 ± .043
21.5	.480 ± .051
21.6	.444 ± .044
22.9	.427 ± .045
23.3	.398 ± .045
27.9	.416 ± .053
28.1	.352 ± .045
28.6	.163 ± .047
30.4	.160 ± .083
31.7	.377 ± .055
31.8	.372 ± .081
31.9	.343 ± .073
35.1	.359 ± .076
35.6	.276 ± .068
36.2	.168 ± .064
36.7	.145 ± .066
36.9	.261 ± .073
37.7	.323 ± .062
40.9	.307 ± .083

The correspondence of these two measures may be indicated by the fact that the Spearman ρ (Thorndike, '04, p. 167; Brown and Thomson, '23, p. 130; Rugg, '17, p. 285) between the two is $-.946$. This figure is high enough to warrant the assumption that the method of overlapping ranks the elements from good to poor in very much the same order as does the bi-serial r, the good elements being defined as those which show low overlappings and high bi-serial correlations.

As a result of this survey of methods, it was decided to use the method of overlapping for the ensuing study of elements. As has been said above (page 5) the intention was to exhaust as nearly as possible the available material. This meant that for some elements there would be many cases, and for others comparatively few. In order to decide the minimum number of cases necessary for reliability, it was thought desirable to measure the reliability of the various frequencies for various levels of difficulty.[6] Kelley ('23, pp. 316 ff.) gives two formulae for the probable error of overlappings, but neither of them applies here, since he assumes independence for the two distributions under consideration; whereas the two distributions from which the overlappings were computed in this study were closely dependent, one being the total test scores for passes on the element, the other, the total test scores for failures.

The most direct method of attacking any reliability measure is to split the data into halves, and to compute the measure to be tested for each half. If the results obtained from the halves check, they would indicate a high reliability for a frequency equal to the number of cases in each half. All of the completion elements with a frequency of 169 (there were 16 of these) were split so that alternate cases of each element fell into each of two halves, 85 cases in one group, and 84 in the other. Reading elements with frequencies ranging from 134 to 150 (there were

---

[6] The level of difficulty had to be weighed as a consideration, because the very easy and the very hard elements present extreme dichotomies. For example, the A's are elements in which the passes are from 97.5 to 98.2 per cent of the total; the H's are those in which the passes are only 5.5 to 8.0 per cent of the total. This means in the case of the H's that the median of the passes must be found from a small group of scores, and the percentage of overlapping failures from a large group of scores. The reverse would be true of the A's, i. e., the median must be computed from a large group, and the overlapping from a small group.

28 of these) were split in the same way into halves of 67 to 75. There were also 12 completion elements with frequencies of 310. These were split into halves of 155. Overlappings were computed for each half of each of these 56 elements. The results are shown in Tables V, VI and VII, from which it can be seen that reliability is largely independent of level of difficulty, and that the overlappings for the paired halves differ a good deal.

If, however, an overlapping of 20 is chosen for the upper limit of goodness, and an overlapping of 35 for the lower limit

TABLE V

COMPLETION

169 CASES SPLIT INTO 84 CASES IN ONE HALF
AND 85 IN THE OTHER HALF

Difficulty of the Element	Omd. for 84 Cases	Omd. for 85 Cases	Omd. for 169 Cases
D	21.4	35.8	25.0
	18.2	30.7	27.1
E	16.2	19.5	12.8
	12.2	23.8	18.5
	33.3	62.1	36.2
F	12.5	33.9	21.2
	12.9	18.5	21.0
	24.1	24.6	24.3
	34.6	40.7	36.7
	24.1	44.0	37.7
G	13.7	16.9	16.0
	*12.3	47.0	19.1
	16.9	21.3	20.9
	20.8	29.3	25.8
	18.8	30.4	26.1
H	9.5	20.2	22.3

Difficulty of Elements	Average Difference Between Halves
D	13.0
E	14.6
F	10.9
G	12.5
H	10.7
Total	12.3

of poorness, there are only five elements (the starred ones) of the 55 whose unreliability would throw them falsely from the good into the poor group, or vice versa. It was after a careful study of these tables and of the ranges of overlappings computed in the later study, that the final basis for selecting the good and poor elements was adopted. This final basis for selection is shown in Table VIII which should be read: If the number of cases from which the overlapping of a completion or reading element was computed is between 50 and 100, an Omd of 0 to 5.4 will classify the element as good; an Omd of 44.5 or more will classify the element as poor, and so forth.

TABLE VI

COMPLETION

310 CASES SPLIT INTO HALVES OF 155

Difficulty of the Element	Omd. for First Half	Omd. for Second Half	Omd. for Total
C	25.0	36.0	27.9
D	20.0	20.5	21.2
	25.4	31.8	28.1
E	28.0	38.6	28.6
F	12.7	19.2	16.5
	22.8	24.3	21.6
	21.5	28.9	22.9
	22.7	22.9	23.3
G	11.9	19.5	15.2
	**3.9	50.3	21.5
H	10.1	17.7	20.7
	**10.9	50.9	20.7

Difficulty of Elements	Average Difference Between Halves
C	11.0
D	3.9
E	10.6
F	3.9
G	27.0
H	23.8
Total	12.2

TABLE VII

READING

134 TO 150 CASES SPLIT INTO HALVES OF 67 TO 75 EACH

Difficulty of the Element	Omd. of First Half	Omd. of Second Half	Omd. of Total
C	0.0	14.0	10.5
	15.4	18.2	12.5
	0.0	16.7	13.3
	5.9	21.4	17.8
	28.0	58.0	35.7
D	0.0	12.0	8.2
	7.1	20.0	13.2
	10.6	26.8	18.6
	12.0	25.0	19.6
	8.7	29.1	23.4
	22.2	24.0	25.4
	27.3	40.0	28.9
	20.7	58.8	33.3
E	5.8	32.5	15.5
	*11.1	36.1	20.8
	17.1	29.1	23.7
	19.5	29.4	27.6
	21.2	36.7	31.1
	25.4	46.1	33.3
	*18.1	62.1	34.1
	28.2	43.4	36.0
	42.5	53.8	47.3
F	7.4	16.0	7.9
	13.0	19.1	15.9
	20.4	23.8	20.4
	19.6	26.7	21.9
	19.6	30.6	23.1
	38.4	51.5	41.0

Difficulty of the Element	Average Difference Between Halves
C	15.8
D	15.9
E	20.0
F	8.2
Total	15.5

TABLE VIII

BASIS FOR SELECTING ELEMENTS AS GOOD OR AS POOR

Frequency for Completion and Reading	Frequency for Arithmetic	This Omd. is Good	This Omd. is Poor
50– 99	50–74	0– 5.4	44.5 or over
100–149	75–99	0–10.4	39.5 or over
150 up	100 up	0–20.4	34.5 or over

Reference to Tables V, VI and VII will show that on this basis only two elements (double star) of the 55 would be classified falsely because of unreliability. These elements fall, one in a G and one in an H level, both more or less extreme dichotomies.

In reading the following chapters, it must be remembered that the overlappings do not point out the more intelligent processes as against the less intelligent. In every case, a good element means an element which differentiates the intelligent from the unintelligent, the high-scored from the low-scored persons. A poor element might be one in which the median of the passes is very high, but in which a number of the failures on the element exceeds even so high a median; or a good element might be one in which the median of the passes is low, but in which practically all of the failures fall below even so low a median.

CHAPTER III

ANALYSIS OF THE COMPLETION ELEMENTS

The completion elements which were chosen as good or as poor were selected, on the basis shown in Table VIII, from the total of 122 completion elements studied. On this basis, 23 elements were accounted good, and 11 poor. In the following discussion a good element, whenever referred to, will mean one of these 23, and a poor element will mean one of the 11. It should be noted that these numbers are not equal, but that the ratio of good elements to poor elements is as 23 to 11. This should be borne in mind in reading the tables and in drawing conclusions from the analyses which follow. In order that the relations of the good elements and of the poor elements with the totals and with each other might be studied, each analysis was applied not only to the good and the poor elements, but to all of the elements for which overlappings had been obtained.

It was to obtain a check on the results of these analysis as well as for light on the type of responses elicited at a different level of development that the data from the sixth grade (or S) group were added to this study. Of the 27 completion elements in this group, 16 were accounted good, and 3 poor.[1]

It must be remembered in reading this chapter that the completion of incomplete sentences is *in itself* a very complex activity, and that any analysis which can be made at the present stage of knowledge about that kind of an activity will probably be inadequate.

---

[1] A different division point, formed upon the same principle as that for the CBL group, was decided upon for this group. The completion test seems to be a somewhat better test for children than for adults, although it is good for both. Trabue's work (Trabue '16) on the completion test was with subjects from grade 2 through college graduation. He says that "the completion of incomplete sentences correlates remarkably well with almost any other measure of desirable qualities." Wyatt ('13, p. 118), who studied completion tests with children from 10 to 13 years of age, says, "The correlation (of completion) is unusually high," and states that correlation as $+ .85$. In McCall's study (McCall, '16, p. 67) with sixth grade children, the Trabue completion test of 28 elements correlated with mental ability $+ .96$.

Table IX gives the distribution of elements and the range of overlappings at each level of difficulty. The proportion of good elements tends to increase as the difficulty increases, except in the H or hardest level and in the C or easiest level.[2] Of particular interest is the fact that goodness, as indicated by low overlappings, is not peculiar to any one level of difficulty but that goodness and poorness both are to be found in all levels.

TABLE IXa

DISTRIBUTION OF COMPLETION ELEMENTS ACCORDING TO DIFFICULTY, AND RANGES OF OVERLAPPING WITHIN EACH LEVEL OF DIFFICULTY

CBL GROUP

Level	Range of Omds.	Good Elements	Poor Elements	Total Elements
H	5.2–61.4	3	3	17
G	9.9–36.4	6	1	30
F	0.0–41.1	5	2	30
E	18.4–55.1	4	3	27
D	16.6–35.8	1	1	9
C	0.0–45.8	4	1	9
Total	....	23	11	122

TABLE IXb

DISTRIBUTION OF COMPLETION ELEMENTS ACCORDING TO DIFFICULTY, AND RANGES OF OVERLAPPING WITHIN EACH LEVEL OF DIFFICULTY

S GROUP

Level	Range of Omds.	Good Elements	Poor Elements	Total Elements
C	7.4–23.0	7	...	9
B	5.1–37.7	6	2	10
A	3.0–44.8	3	1	8
Total	....	16	3	27

There is a tendency for the good elements to be longer than the poor elements. The average length of the 122 completions in

---

[2] The H level seems to furnish exceptions to general tendencies throughout the analyses of reading and arithmetic as well as of the completion elements. The lack of numbers in the cases of extreme ease or difficulty may explain these exceptions, or it may be that the H elements are so hard that chance enters as a factor in passing them. The extreme dichotomy in the computation of the overlapping is also a factor.

the CBL group was 1.56 lines; of the good CBL completions, 1.60 lines, and of the poor CBL completions, 1.50 lines. This tendency becomes more marked in the S group in which the average length of all completion elements was .88 lines; of the good elements, .98 lines; and of the poor, .53 lines. This tendency still remained when the levels of difficulty were held constant.

There is a clear tendency for the good elements to be those with more omissions. This is probably to be expected, since the good elements are the longer ones. The average number of omissions for the 122 CBL completion elements was 4.42; for the 23 good elements, 5.96; and for the poor elements, 4.27. For the S group, the average number of omissions for the total was 2.18; for the good elements, 2.70; and for the poor elements, 1.33. The tendency remained when the levels of difficulty were held constant.

An analysis was made on the basis of the content of the sentences to be completed. Such sentences as the following were classified as requiring special *information* for their completion.

1. Divisor times quotient will .... dividend, if the .... is done correctly.
2. Few historians would .... the fact that Marx had a larger and more thorough .... on the social .... of his time .... any .... living man.

Another type was made up of maxims and *philosophical* sentences, such as:

1. Not .... persons are eager to work hard.
2. They who are miserable have .... medicine other .... hope.
3. No .... is powerful .... to .... two and two be five.

The *ordinary* sentences were like these:

1. He will come .... he is not ill.
2. .... you wish me to help you .... Latin, please .... me by telephone.

The results showed that the information type of sentence was good for the higher (F, G and H) levels of the CBL group, but poor for the lower levels, and indifferent for the S group. The reverse was true of the philosophical content. It was good for the lower levels of the CBL group, and for the S group.

The completion elements were analyzed into parts of speech, each blank having been filled in with the best scored answer from the key, and these words classified.[3] The results showed the following facts:

1. All omissions, except passive intransitive verbs and indefinite pronouns, were good for the S group. There were, however, no coordinating conjunctions, prepositions of time or place, past or present participles, or abstract nouns among the 58 omissions in this group.

2. In the CBL group:

Nouns showed no constant tendency.

Pronouns were good for levels D and E, especially personal pronouns (which were especially favored by the S group also).

Verbs showed no constant tendency.

Adjectives were fairly good throughout, excepting for level D.

Adverbs were very good, especially for the lower levels. (The S group also showed adverbs to be especially good.)

Prepositions were very good, especially for the lower levels.

Conjunctions: Coordinating were good for levels F and G (did not appear in C and D). Subordinating were good for F and G.

Participles were good for all levels except C, where they did not appear, and D, where there was only one case which was classified as neither good nor poor.

Articles showed no constant tendency.

In summary: The nouns, verbs, and articles showed no constant tendencies; conjunctions were good for the higher levels; participles and adjectives were good except for the lower levels; prepositions and adverbs were good throughout, especially in the lower levels.

Among the 122 CBL elements, there were fourteen which had blanks at the beginning of the sentence. Of these, four were among the best five of the good elements; none of the fourteen were among the poor elements, although ten were classified as neither good nor poor. Among the S elements, there were four which had blanks at the beginning of the sentence. All four of these were good elements. This might lead to the assumption that the initiation of a thought process is a more intelligent per-

---

[3] The writer is indebted to Miss Ruth Andrus for help with this analysis. Miss Andrus has been a teacher and thorough student of ancient and modern languages for a number of years.

formance than the mere continuation of a process once initiated. An analysis of these beginning blanks into parts of speech showed nothing.

In order to study the relations between difficulty, goodness, and content, coefficients of contingency (Yule, '22, pp. 64 ff.) were computed. The levels of difficulty were six in number, C, D, E, F, G, and H, for the CBL group, and three in number, A, B, and C, for the S group. The types of content were three, informational, philosophical, and ordinary. The goodness, as measured by overlappings, was broken up into categories of 10 per cent each, from 0 to 9.9, 10 to 19.9, etc. The coefficients are given in Table X.

TABLE X
CONTINGENCY COEFFICIENTS FOR COMPLETION ELEMENTS

	CBL Group	S Group
Goodness and Difficulty	.302	.525
Goodness and Content	.242	.417
Difficulty and Content	.118	.457

Content held constant; Goodness and Difficulty for content of:

	CBL Group	S Group
Information	.603	.627
Philosophy	.609	.612
Ordinary	.556	.736
Average	.589	.658

Difficulty held constant; Goodness and Content for difficulty:

	CBL Group		S Group
H	.621	C	.641
G	.506	B	.495
F	.505	A	.707
E	.477		
D	.542	Average	.614
C	.599		
Average	.542		

There is a definite relation between goodness and difficulty, especially for the S group. When content is held constant, this relation becomes marked for both groups. The same is true of goodness and content, when difficulty is held constant. Goodness, it seems apparent, is more or less closely related to some factor which has not been analyzed out.

CHAPTER IV

ANALYSIS OF READING ELEMENTS

It is true of the reading elements, as well as of the completion elements, that an analysis must be subjective in some of its phases. The reading tests used in this study consisted of a number of paragraphs, each having a series of questions to be answered.[1]

Table XI shows how the elements were distributed within the various levels of difficulty. The number of good, the number of poor, and the total number of elements, as well as the range of overlappings within each level, are given.

TABLE XI

DISTRIBUTION OF ELEMENTS AND RANGES OF OVERLAPPINGS
FOR LEVELS OF DIFFICULTY IN READING

Level	Range of Omds.	Number of Good Elements	Number of Poor Elements	Total Number of Elements
H	10.9–23.8	...	...	4
G	10.4–43.6	2	...	11
F	7.9–50.0	4	4	24
E	13.5–47.3	2	4	33
D	4.3–50.0	10	3	30
C	9.5–75.0	5	2	14
B	0.0–33.3	1	...	3
A	All taking it passed	...	2	2
Total	....	24	15	121

Levels C and D contain the highest proportion of good elements. There are many factors other than difficulty, however, which make for goodness in reading. Note that in reading, as in completion, there are various levels of goodness within each level of difficulty.

There were three possibilities for the form in which the answers to the questions were made, namely, (1) the yes-no type; (2) the alternate response type; and (3) free or essay type.

---

[1] Three copies of the actual elements studied have been deposited in the Bryson Library of Teachers College.

TABLE XII

DISTRIBUTION OF GOODNESS ACCORDING TO
FORM OF RESPONSE

Form of Response	Number* Good	Number* Poor	Total Number*	Average Omd.
Yes-No	2	1	10	28.3
Alternate.........	1	4	15	31.7
Free.............	24	18	12	25.7

* These numbers do not check those of Table XI, because in some elements two responses were expected, which, if of different forms, had to be classified under two different heads.

The results (Table XII) point to the poorness of the alternate response forms, and to the goodness of the free and yes-no forms in the order mentioned. These results cannot, however, be considered conclusive, since 81.8 per cent of all possible answers were of the free response form, and since the *smallness of the difference* was more prominent than the *fact of difference.*

Probably the most important difference between good and poor elements came from an analysis into types of response. Five types were decided upon as follows:

1. Responses which required organization of, and inference from, the material given in the paragraph. These were cases in which the material necessary for answering the question was not directly embodied in the paragraph, but in which the answer to the question must have been inferred. A question of this type is, "What do you think was the topic of the paragraph preceding this, in the book whence this paragraph was taken?"

2. The second type of response was called "general organization." These were responses requiring organization of material which could not be easily located in the paragraph by a key word or phrase. This type stands in contrast with type 3, described below. An example of type 2 is, "What is the main fact asserted in this paragraph?"

3. The third type of response was that in which organization was necessary, but organization of only one or two sentences which could be easily located by a key word or phrase in the question asked. These (and cases of type 5) were cases in which the question could have been answered by locating such a key word or phrase in the paragraph, and reading around it. They were elements which could have been answered without having

read the whole paragraph. The following paragraph and question illustrate this type:

The body of legal rules and customs which obtained in England before the Norman conquest constitutes, with the Scandinavian laws, the most genuine expression of Teutonic legal thought. While the so-called "barbaric laws" of the continent, not excepting those in the territory now called Germany, were largely the product of Roman influence, the continuity of Roman life was almost completely broken in the island, and even the Church, the direct heir of Roman tradition, did not carry on a continuous existence: Canterbury was not a see formed in a Roman province in the same sense as Tours or Reims. One of the striking expressions of this Teutonism is presented by the language in which the Anglo-Saxons laws were written. They are uniformly worded in English, while continental laws, apart from the Scandinavian, are all in Latin. The English dialect in which the Anglo-Saxon laws have been handed down to us is in most cases a common speech derived from West Saxon— naturally enough as Wessex became the predominant English state, and the court of its kings the principal literary center from which most of the compilers and scribes derived their dialect and spelling. Traces of Kentish speech may be detected, however, in the *Textus Roffensis,* the MS. of the Kentish laws; the Northumbrian dialectical peculiarities are also noticeable on some occasions, while Danish words occur only as technical terms.

Question: What reason is given for the use of the particular dialect in which most of the Anglo-Saxon laws were written?

4 and 5. The fourth and fifth types of response represented cases in which a direct quotation of a sentence or phrase in the paragraph would have answered the question satisfactorily. (4) is to be distinguished from (5) by the fact that in (4) the sentence or phrase to be copied could not have been located without organization of, or inference from, the material in the paragraph; whereas in (5) the usable quotation could have been easily located by scanning the paragraph for a key word or phrase. Examples of (4) and (5) follow in sequence:

Example of (4): *Sapphire,* a blue transparent variety of corundum, or native alumina, much valued as a gem-stone. It is essentially the same mineral as ruby, from which it differs chiefly in color. The color of the normal sapphire varies from the palest blue to the deepest indigo, the most esteemed tint being that of the blue cornflower. Many of the crystals are parti-colored, the blue being distributed in patches in a colorless or yellow stone; but by skillful cutting, the deep-colored portion may be caused to impart color to the entire gem. As the sapphire crystallizes in the hexagonal system it is dichoric, but in pale stones this character may not be well marked. In a deep colored stone the color may be resolved, by the dichroscope, into an ultramarine blue and a bluish or yellowish green.

Question: How may a stone showing local chromatic variations be made to appear deep-colored throughout?

Example of (5): *Sale* is commonly defined as the transfer of property from one person to another for a price. The definition requires some consideration in order to appreciate its full scope. The law of sale is usually treated as a branch of the law of contract, because sale is effected by contract. But a complicated contract of sale is something more. It is a contract plus a transfer of property. An agreement to sell or buy a thing, or, as lawyers call it, an executory contract of sale, is a contract pure and simple. A purely personal bond arises thereby between seller and buyer. But a complete or executed contract of sale effects a transfer of ownership with all the advantages and risks incident thereto. By an agreement to sell a *jus in personam* is created; by a sale a *jus in rem* is transferred.

Question: Under what department of law does the law regarding sales come?

In addition to these five classes of response, it was necessary to take consideration of the case in which two or more facts in the paragraph competed for attention, cases in which the answer to the element question was obscured by too many facts crowded into a short space. There are six cases of this kind. Of the six, one proved to be an especially good element; the other five were all poor.

An analysis of the reading elements into five categories such as those described, was of necessity a subjective analysis. In order to make it as objective as possible, the writer classified the elements once on each of five different days. The analyses of the fourth and fifth days checked so closely that further repetition of the process was considered unnecessary. In cases of doubt as to how the elements should have been classified (this procedure was followed in the case of the arithmetic and completion elements also), the advice of from two to five other persons was asked, and a final decision arrived at in that way. Table XIII gives the results of the analysis into types of response.

From Table XIII it is seen that Type 1, Inference, was good throughout the levels of difficulty. Type (2), General Organization, was not so good. The reason probably lay in the fact that all six of the cases (one of them good, the other five poor) which were classified as having "competing facts" were of the general organization type, and furnished five of the six poor elements under that head. They were distributed as follows: 1 B,

TABLE XIII

DISTRIBUTION OF ELEMENTS ACCORDING TO
TYPES OF RESPONSE IN READING

Level	Numbers in	Type 1, Inference	Type 2, General Organization	Type 3, Organization Easily Located	Type 4, Quotation Located by Organization	Type 5, Quotation Easily Located
H .... Good		..	..	..	..	..
Poor		..	..	..	..	..
Total		..	2	1	..	1
G .... Good		1	1	..	1	..
Poor		..	..	..	..	..
Total		8	2	2	2	..
F .... Good		4	1	..	..	..
Poor		..	2	..	..	1
Total		9	5	3	4	4
E .... Good		..	1	1	..	..
Poor		..	1	1	1	1
Total		7	7	4	11	5
D .... Good		3	2	..	3	1
Poor		1	3	..	..	2
Total		8	7	2	7	7
C .... Good		1	1	..	1	2
Poor		..	..	1	1	..
Total		2	1	2	4	7
B .... Good		..	1	..	..	..
Poor		..	..	..	..	..
Total		1	1	..	..	..
A .... Good		..	..	..	..	..
Poor		..	..	..	..	2
Total		..	..	..	..	2
Total*.... Good		9	7	1	5	3
Poor		1	6	2	2	6
Total		35	25	14	28	26

* These totals do not check Table XI for the same reason that Table XII does not check it, and for the added reason that an occasional element could not properly be classed under any of these five heads.

2 D's, 1 E, 2 F's. Type 3, Organization Easily Located, claimed 14 elements (or parts of elements), 1 of which was good, 2 poor. Type 4, Quotation Requiring Organization to Locate, was more good than poor; and Type 5, Quotation Easily Located, was markedly poor.

If˙these types are taken in combination, it can be seen that Types 1, 2, and 4 as against Types 3 and 5 give the most noticeable difference; for, of the 88 elements in the (1), (2), (4) combination (Types 1, 2, and 4), 21 were good, and 9 poor; whereas of the 40 elements in the combination of Types 3 and 5, 4 only

TABLE XIV
COEFFICIENTS OF CONTINGENCY FOR THE READING ELEMENTS

Type of Response and Difficulty = .474
Goodness and Type of Response = .308
Goodness and Difficulty   = .552

With Type of Response constant, the coefficients for Goodness and Difficulty for each type are:

$$
\begin{aligned}
I &= .665 \\
II &= .729 \\
III &= .740 \\
IV &= .571 \\
V &= .638
\end{aligned}
$$

Average = .668

With levels of Difficulty constant, the coefficients for Goodness and Type for each level are:

$$
\begin{aligned}
H &= .542 \\
G &= .701 \\
F &= .619 \\
E &= .615 \\
D &= .493 \\
C &= .748
\end{aligned}
$$

Average = .6197, or .620.

were good, and 8 were poor. *In reading elements, then, the discriminating factor was not form of answer* (organization as against quotation), *but the type of organization necessary in order to arrive at the answer.*

An analysis of the paragraphs into types of subject matter was made. There was a tendency for the professional and scientific subject matter to furnish more good elements than did the cultural (history, literature, music, etc.), although the differences were small, and probably outweighed by other factors in goodness or poorness. This smallness of difference is especially noticeable in the fact that a number of the paragraphs furnished both good and poor, as well as indifferent, elements.

Since the relationships between goodness, difficulty, and types of response seemed to be close, the contingency coefficients were worked out with five categories in types of response, with six levels of difficulty (A and B omitted, because of the small frequencies; H should probably have been omitted also), and with goodness measured as in completion, in intervals of 10 per cents of overlapping. The coefficients may be found in Table XIV.

CHAPTER V

ANALYSIS OF THE ARITHMETIC ELEMENTS

There were 131 arithmetic elements studied from the CBL group, and 43 (23 of them the same as from the CBL group) from the S group. Table XV shows how the good and poor elements, and the ranges of overlappings were distributed within each level of difficulty. A clear relationship between goodness and difficulty is evident. Again, as for reading and completion, there is a wide range of overlappings at each level of difficulty.

The question as to the relation between difficulty and complexity was raised. In order to answer it, the arithmetic elements

TABLE XVa
DISTRIBUTION OF GOOD AND POOR ELEMENTS AND
RANGE OF OVERLAPPINGS FOR ARITHMETIC
CBL GROUP

Difficulty	Good	Poor	Total	Range of Omds.
H	. . .	. . .	2	31.6–34.7
G	12	1	20	10.4–37.0
F	9	1	29	7.4–38.9
E	7	2	25	9.8–44.7
D	. . .	3	25	12.5–66.7
C	3	6	16	17.7–50.0
B	. . .	5	9	16.7–50.0
A	2	1	5	0.0–66.7
Total	33	19	131	

TABLE XVb
DISTRIBUTION OF GOOD AND POOR ELEMENTS AND
RANGE OF OVERLAPPINGS FOR ARITHMETIC
S GROUP

Difficulty	Good	Poor	Total	Range of Omds.
D	1	1	6	9.2–34.2
C	8	3	17	3.6–33.3
AA*.....	7	3	10	0.0–34.3
AAA*.....	5	2	10	14.2–43.4
Total	21	9	43	

* Easier than the Columbia A's.

were analyzed from the point of view of complexity. Such an analysis was possible with the arithmetic element because there was at least one objective measure of complexity, namely, the number of processes or operations necessary in order to arrive at the answer of the problem. Even this must, of course, be somewhat arbitrary. It was decided to call multiplication or division by a fraction, with a numerator more than 1, a double process; if necessary to reduce a mixed number to a fraction in order to work with it, this was called one process. On the other hand, multiplication or division by any number, no matter how many digits it contained, was considered as a single process. Since the problems were scored in the test as correct whether fractions in answers were reduced to their lowest terms or not, this analysis was carried only as far as unreduced answers. Sample analyses are given to make clear what was done at this point.

I. Problem: At 15c a yard, how much will 7 feet of cloth cost?

Analysis 1
(1) 3 feet = 1 yard
(2) 7 feet = 7/3 yards
(3) 1 yard costs 15c; 1/3 yard costs 5c
(4) 7/3 yards cost 35c

Analysis 2
(1) 1 yard = 3 feet
(2) 15c for 3 feet; 5c for 1 foot
(3) 7 × 5 = 35c for 7 feet.

In this, as in all cases, the simplest analysis that could be worked out was taken. This problem was called a 3-process problem.

II. Problem:

3D cost 25c; 4J cost 25c
1J costs .... as much as 1D.

Analysis 1
(1) 1J costs 1/4 as much as 4J
(2) 1/4 of 25c = 25/4 cents
(3) 1D costs 1/3 as much as 3D
(4) 1/3 of 25c = 25/3 cents
(5) 25/4 = 75/12
(6) 25/3 = 100/12
(7) 75/12 = 3/4 of 100/12

Analysis 2
(1) 4J cost the same as 3D
(2) 1J costs 1/4 as much as 3D
(3) 1J costs 1/4 divided by 1/3 or 3/4 as much as 1D.

It is quite possible that the writer has not always arrived at the simplest analysis of all of the problems. A sincere effort was made to do so, and in the measure that simplicity was not reached, this analysis is at fault.

There was an occasional problem in which pure reasoning would have obtained an answer. For example, "What number doubled

TABLE XVIa

DISTRIBUTION OF ELEMENTS IN THE VARIOUS DEGREES OF
COMPLEXITY OF ARITHMETIC PROBLEMS
CBL GROUP

Level of Difficulty		Processes									
		1	2	3	4	5	6	7	8	9	10
H	Good	..	..	..	..	..	..	..	..	..	..
	Poor	..	..	..	..	..	..	..	..	..	..
	Total	..	..	..	..	1	..	..	1	..	..
G	Good	1	1	2	2	..	1	2	1	1	1
	Poor	1	..	..	..	..	..	..	..	..	..
	Total	2	1	2	3	2	2	4	2	1	1
F	Good	..	3	4	..	..	1	..	..	..	..
	Poor	..	1	..	..	..	..	..	..	..	..
	Total	3	6	10	3	2	3	..	1	..	..
E	Good	2	2	1	2	..	..	..	..	..	..
	Poor	1	..	1	..	..	..	..	..	..	..
	Total	6	5	9	4	1	..	..	..	..	..
D	Good	..	..	..	..	..	..	..	..	..	..
	Poor	1	2	..	..	..	..	..	..	..	..
	Total	6	12	4	..	..	..	..	..	..	..
C	Good	1	1	..	..	..	1	..	..	..	..
	Poor	2	4	..	..	..	..	..	..	..	..
	Total	3	5	3	3	..	1	1	..	..	..
B	Good	..	..	..	..	..	..	..	..	..	..
	Poor	1	3	..	..	..	..	..	..	..	..
	Total	1	6	..	..	..	..	..	..	..	..
A	Good	2	..	..	..	..	..	..	..	..	..
	Poor	1	..	..	..	..	..	..	..	..	..
	Total	5	..	..	..	..	..	..	..	..	..
Total	Good	6	7	7	4	..	3	2	1	1	1
	Poor	7	10	1	..	..	..	..	..	..	..
	Total	26	35	28	13	6	6	5	4	1	1

TABLE XVIb

Level of Difficulty		Processes									
		1	2	3	4	5	6	7	8	9	10
D	Good	..	1	..	..	..	..	..	..	..	..
	Poor	..	1	..	..	..	..	..	..	..	..
	Total	1	5	..	..	..	..	..	..	..	..
C	Good	1	2	1	3	..	..	1	..	..	..
	Poor	1	2	..	..	..	..	..	..	..	..
	Total	3	5	4	3	..	1	1	..	..	..
AA	Good	4	3	..	..	..	..	..	..	..	..
	Poor	1	1	1	..	..	..	..	..	..	..
	Total	5	4	1	..	..	..	..	..	..	..
AAA	Good	1	4	..	..	..	..	..	..	..	..
	Poor	2	..	..	..	..	..	..	..	..	..
	Total	3	7	..	..	..	..	..	..	..	..
Total	Good	6	10	1	3	..	..	1	..	..	..
	Poor	4	4	1	..	..	..	..	..	..	..
	Total	12	21	5	3	..	1	1	..	..	..

equals 2 times 3?" Such problems were not included in the
analysis for complexity. Table XVI gives the results. It shows
a clear relationship between difficulty and complexity, the more
complex problems tending to be the more difficult ones in both
the CBL and the S groups. From the row of totals, it becomes
evident that the relationship between goodness and complexity is
also close. No problem which required more than three processes
for its solution proved to be a poor element, and only one problem
in each group which required more than two processes, proved
to be poor.

The coefficients of contingency for the various relations between difficulty, complexity, and goodness were computed. Categories which contained too few cases were omitted. Table XVII
gives these coefficients.

TABLE XVII

CONTINGENCY COEFFICIENTS FOR THE ARITHMETIC ELEMENTS

	CBL	S
Complexity and Difficulty	.700	.329
Goodness and Difficulty	.662	.345
Goodness and Complexity	.545	.572

Difficulty constant: coefficients between Goodness and Complexity at levels:

CBL	S
G = .725	D = .408
F = .607	C = .771
E = .480	AA = .581
D = .561	AAA = .494
C = .751	
Average = .625	Average = .564

Complexity constant: coefficients between Goodness and Difficulty for number of processes:

Processes	CBL	Processes	S
8 =	.707 (4 cases)	3 =	.707
7 =	.241	2 =	.443
6 =	.500	1 =	.639
5 =	.632		
4 =	.638	Average =	.596
3 =	.691		
2 =	.703		
1 =	.824		
Average =	.617		

Although complexity and difficulty are closely related, they are apparently not the same thing, since the partial coefficients of each when the other is held constant are relatively high.

An analysis into kinds of processes necessary for solution was made. By a "kind of process" is meant multiplication or division by a simple fraction, by a compound fraction, or by a simple whole number, and so on. The results showed nothing of note, except that all of the types of processes were better in the upper levels of difficulty than in the lower levels, and that no process was notably better than any other. One fact alone showed clearly, and upon investigation stood out. The relational types of problem were much superior to any other general type of problem or process. Example II of problem analyses (page 29) is an example of this type. Of the 131 problems studied, 50 were classed as of this type. Of these, 13 were good and none were poor; only 4 had an overlapping higher than 30.0.

An analysis of the form in which the problems were stated was made.   Three possibilities were considered:

I. The completion form.
   (1) ¼ of 16 = ½ of ....
   (2) If E costs 10c each, and G costs 40c per lb., 3E costs ....
       as much as ½ lb. G.

II. The simple statement form.
   (1) What number doubled is half of eight?
   (2) How many times as long as 8 ft. is 12 yds.?

III. The problem statement.
   (1) One quart of ice cream is enough for 5 persons.   How many
       quarts will be enough for 15 persons?

Form made practically no difference in the CBL group, but the S group discriminated against the completion form in favor of the problem statement.   It is possible that with children the solving of problems has not yet become mechanical to the point where form of statement makes no difference, and that the problem statement, being the form to which they are accustomed, measures discriminatingly, whereas completion, being a new form, allows chance to figure.   If this is a legitimate explanation of the facts, it offers further proof of the accepted hypothesis that an abstract mental process can become free of the mechanical form in which the material dealt with is presented.

CHAPTER VI

CONCLUSIONS

1. The method of overlapping is the most practicable of the methods studied for dealing with test elements. Its only competitor is the method of the bi-serial r. The two methods rank elements from good to poor in much the same order ($\rho = -.946$); the computation of the overlapping necessitates the expenditure of much less time, and thus makes possible in a given period the study of many more elements.

2. There is a clear positive relationship between the goodness of an element and the difficulty of that element. This does not mean, however, that goodness is peculiar to the difficult elements, for goodness and poorness can be found at all levels of difficulty.

3. There is a clear positive relationship between the goodness of an element and the complexity of that element. This is shown by the relationship between goodness and length, and between goodness and number of omissions in completion; between goodness and type of response in reading; and between goodness and number of processes in arithmetic. As with difficulty, goodness is not peculiar to the more complex elements. Simple elements occasionally discriminate between the intelligent and the unintelligent quite as well as do the more complex elements.

4. Complexity and difficulty tend to accompany one another. The coefficient of contingency for the CBL group in arithmetic was .700. The partial contingency coefficients, however (coefficient for goodness and difficulty with complexity constant $= .617$; for goodness and complexity with difficulty constant $= .625$), show that complexity and difficulty are not the same thing.

5. The specific content of elements (professional as against cultural in reading, informational as against philosophical in completion) bears some relationship to goodness. It seems quite possible, however, that the personnel of the CBL group (Columbia and Law in excess of Barnard) may account for a large part of this relationship.

6. The form in which elements are presented has a slight effect upon their goodness with adults, a more noticeable effect with children. Forms of presentation which are familiar to children discriminate between intelligent and unintelligent children better than do unfamiliar forms.

7. Types of elements which discriminate between the intelligent and the unintelligent at one level of difficulty, do not always so discriminate at other levels. In the construction of measuring scales, it is desirable, according to most authorities, to have represented in each scale many levels of difficulty. This study offers a caution to the makers of scales in the statement that what discriminates at one level may not and frequently does not do so at other levels. It is left to the theory of scale construction to apply this fact.

8. The work in analysis of test elements has only begun. Methods of attack are still far from perfect and offer a most interesting field for investigation. Perfection of methods and detailed analyses of test elements should be of invaluable assistance to the ultimate perfection of tests and scales.

BIBLIOGRAPHY

Brown and Thomson ('23). *Essentials of Mental Measurements.* Cambridge University Press.

Burt ('09). "Experimental Tests of General Intelligence." *British Journal of Psychology,* Vol. III.

Ebbinghaus ('97). "Uber eine neue Methode zur Prüfung geistiger Fähigkeiten und ihre Anwendung bei Schulkindern." *Zeitschrift für Psychologie,* Vol. 13. Quoted from Trabue.

Gates and La Salle ('23). "Relative Predictive Values of Certain Intelligence and Educational Tests Together with a Study of the Effect of Educational Achievement upon Intelligence Test Scores." *Journal of Educational Psychology,* Dec., 1923.

Herring ('24). *Revision of the Binet Simon Tests and Verbal and Abstract Elements in Intelligence Examinations.* World Book Company.

Kelley ('14). *Educational Guidance.* Teachers College Contributions to Education, No. 71.

Kelley ('23). *Statistical Method.* Macmillan Company.

McCall ('16). *Correlation of Some Psychological and Educational Measurements.* Teachers College Contributions to Education, No. 79.

Plato. Translated by Jowett ('88). Oxford Clarendon Press.

Rugg ('17). *Statistical Methods Applied to Education.* Houghton Mifflin Co.

Spearman and Hart ('12). "General Ability, Its Existence and Nature." *British Journal of Psychology,* Vol. V.

Stern ('12). Translated by Whipple ('14). *The Psychological Methods of Testing Intelligence.* Educational Psychology Monographs, No. 13.

Thorndike ('04). *Mental and Social Measurements.* Teachers College.

Trabue ('16). *Completion-Test Language Scales.* Teachers College Contributions to Education, No. 77.

Wood ('23). *Measurement in Higher Education.* World Book Co.

Woodworth ('22). *Dynamic Psychology.* Columbia University Press.

Wyatt ('13). "The Quantitative Measurement of Higher Mental Processes." *British Journal of Psychology,* Vol. VI, Part I.

Yule ('22). *An Introduction to the Theory of Statistics.* C. Griffin and Co.